CHELTENHAM
IN OLD PHOTOGRAPHS
A SECOND SELECTION

CYRIL PALMER on his home-made 7 ft. tall carnival motorbike, 1934.

CHELTENHAM
IN OLD PHOTOGRAPHS
A SECOND SELECTION

COLLECTED BY
ROGER WHITING

Budding
BOOKS

A Budding Book

First published in 1988 by Alan Sutton Publishing Limited

This edition published in 2000 by Budding Books,
an imprint of Sutton Publishing Limited
Phoenix Mill · Thrupp · Stroud · Gloucestershire GL5 2BU

A catalogue record for this book is available from the British Library

ISBN 1-84015-148-X

Typesetting and origination by
Sutton Publishing Limited.
Printed in Great Britain by
Redwood Books, Trowbridge, Wiltshire

CONTENTS

Other books by Dr Whiting published
by Alan Sutton Publishing Ltd:

A Handful of History
A House of Correction
Cheltenham in Old Photographs, volume 1
The Enterprise of England: The Spanish Armada

INTRODUCTION

So many Cheltonians bought the first volume of *Cheltenham in Old Photographs* that the opportunity of producing another volume to fill in the gaps was tempting. So here it is. The section on 'Streets and Buildings' has enabled me to fill in a number of gaps in the survey of the town and its immediate surroundings not covered in Volume 1. I was delighted to find another picture of boating on Liddington Lake, among many other discoveries. Other enchanting pictures are those of the mill and a half-timbered house. Charlton Lawn in 1914 provides an opportunity of showing both the gentry and servants connected with this fine house. 'Shops and Industries' opens with a series on the firm of H.H. Martyn which should prove fascinating. The breadth of work carried out by the firm is staggering. Among the bicycle shop pictures, notice the one offering to give riding lessons. Woodward's piano delivery by horse-drawn cart is interesting, as are those on shaving saloons.

'Transport' continues to offer a wide variety of material, particularly with regard to coaches. I was surprised to find that pre-war coaches had toilets in them. One wonders why they were omitted for so many years after World War II! Rather like the putting of toilets in prison cells in the nineteenth century, only to remove them in the twentieth. In 'Events' I have aimed to produce a wide cross section of material, from the serious to the ridiculous.

A new section in this volume is the one on 'Churches and Chapels'. You may find it surprising to see so many photographs of sports teams proudly presented with their clergy. In the nineteenth century the public schools, of which Cheltenham had its fill, developed the concept of 'muscular Christianity', that is, using organised games to develop the healthy mind believed to be a basic essential of the Christian citizen. In due course this led to 'public school' clergy starting football teams for their young, otherwise deprived, parishioners. But the outcome was a devotion to sport as an end in itself, rather than a means to an end.

'People' covers an exceptionally wide range in this volume. From working men's clubs to society weddings, and from numerous scout and guide activities to the local Rabbit Club. Ladies' hats and men's caps abound!

When you look at the formal photographs of pupils in their classrooms, notice how the teachers have often taken up a 'protective' position at the sides or back of their classes. The camera, with its dramatic flash system, could still be an awe-inspiring gadget. Perhaps that is why team coaches sometimes take up a similar pose alongside football teams.

In the section on the 'Two World Wars' I have included quite a number of pictures from the 1940s to show how steps were taken by the people of Cheltenham to face up to another war, just as they had to the first one. Particularly interesting, after Volume 1's survey of World War I emergency hospitals, are the set on the American hospital at Ullenwood. A much better photograph of the World War I tank at Westal Green appears in this section too, as does a World War II photograph with a modern gun between the famous Sebastopol guns.

'Sport' opens with a selection on swimming in which the town has a proud record. Motorcycle football is one of the more unusual sports to find its place in this volume. I have been pleased to include a much larger section on 'Entertainment' this time. This was simply due to the fact that people came forward with photographs for this volume, whereas as appeals for such photographs last time had produced little. So my thanks to their owners. Subjects covered range from orchestras to pierrots, and cinemas to performing birds. Individuals, groups and societies all offer their talents and are justly commemorated by these old photographs.

Cheltenham possesses a wonderful collection of photographs covering the first half of this century in the past numbers of the *Cheltenham Chronicle and Gloucestershire Graphic*. Bound copies of this weekly picture paper can be seen in the Reference Libraries in Cheltenham and Gloucester.

Finally my thanks to all who helped me to compile this book are recorded in 'Acknowledgements'. I hope readers will find this book both instructive and enjoyable. I trust that it will encourage them to keep photographs which might, in half a century's time, be wanted for another book like this one. If so, please record the date, place and people concerned on the back of your photographs before you forget!

SECTION ONE

Streets and Buildings

PITTVILLE LAKE, no date.

LECKHAMPTON COURT ENTRANCE WITH THE ORIGINAL PITTVILLE GATES, about 1907.

ROTUNDA, no date.

CHELTENHAM SPA MEDICAL BATHS.

WHY GO AWAY WHEN YOU CAN BE TREATED HERE ?

ombieres: For Colitis and Intestinal Disorders.
Vichy Douche: For Goutiness, Toxaemia, Obesity, Arthritis, Fibrositis.
Paraffin Wax: For Lumbago, Myositis, Fibrositis, Stif Adhesions in Wounds, etc.

CHELTENHAM SPA MEDICAL BATHS, 1924. Top row, left to right, Plombieres: for Colitis and Intestinal Disorders; Vichy Douche: for Gout, Toxaemia, Obesity, Arthritis, Fibrositis; Paraffin Wax: for Lumbago, Myositis, Stiff Joints. Bottom row, Contrast: for Vaso-Motor Affections, Foot Swellings, Chilblains; Aerated Whirlpool: for Neurasthenia, Shell-Shock; Radient Light and Heat: for Neuritis, Lumbago, Rheumatism; Sedative Pool: for Sleeplessness, Chronic Rheumatism, Chronic Alcoholism. Also available were Radio-Active Mud Baths 'in great demand for Treatment of Rheumatoid Arthritis'. T. Allan-Burns was then the Spa Manager.

LANSDOWN HOTEL, CHELTENHAM, 1940.

THE CRIMEAN WAR GUNS outside the Queen's Hotel.

THE NEW OR GENTLEMEN'S CLUB on the Promenade, where the Quadrangle is today, c. 1906.

IMPERIAL SPA BUILDING when it was used by the Cheltenham (later Gloucestershire) Dairy in around 1910. The building originally stood on the site of the Queen's Hotel before being moved to the Promenade, behind the fountain.

INTERIOR OF THE IMPERIAL SPA BUILDING when it was used by the Cheltenham Dairy for teas and as a dancing school.

ROYAL CRESCENT in the old days.

THE COLONNADE SHOPPING PRECINCT in the Lower Promenade, c. 1903.

HIGH STREET, CHELTENHAM, 1908.

BELLE VUE HOTEL, High Street, 1912.

PRESTBURY ROAD with H.A. Bustin's *Ye Old Prestbury Road Stores*, which he claimed had been 'established nearly 100 years'. Probably in the 1920s.

TENNYSON ROAD, bus terminus at St Mark's, c. 1934.

THE GAS WORKS AND OFFICES, Gloucester Road, 1917.

LOWER ALSTON MILL at the corner of Mill Street and Six Chimney Lane, with the Gas Works on the right. Tom Phillips, the miller, is shown in this photograph taken c. 1902.

TUDOR COTTAGE, Gloucester Road, originally known as *The Old Farm*. It stood between the Central School and the Gas Works, but now stands at the entrance to Rossley Manor. This photograph was taken in June, 1928.

GLOUCESTER ROAD POST OFFICE as it was between 1888 and 1915. It is now the Calcutta Inn.

SANDFORD PARK, just before its official opening in 1927. The stream was a new feature.

GENERAL HOSPITAL, no date.

MR HOWELL'S GARDEN on what is now the Rodney Road car-park site. Mr Howell, a surgeon and mayor of Cheltenham, lived in Imperial Square, but as his house had no garden he had this separate one, c. 1912.

LIDDINGTON LAKE AND PLEASURE GARDENS, c. 1908. The proprietress, Mrs Lewis, advertised that the lake was only 3 ft. deep and that a good day's fishing (roach, perch, tench, carp, eels) could be had for 6d. The Gardens were open from Easter Monday to 1 November and after that skating was 6d when the lake was frozen. The 10 ft. steam boat was moved to Pittville Lake in around 1910, where it nearly blew up on its first trip.

NAUNTON PARK ENTRANCE. Notice the way 'Naunton Park' has been woven into the archway.

NAUNTON PARK, with the almshouses in the background and the drinking fountain in the foreground, c. 1907.

CLEEVE HILL, no date.

MISS ETHEL AND MISS MURIEL BERKELEY with their pony, 'Bobby', outside Charlton Lawn at the turn of the century.

CHARLTON LAWN AT COP'S ELM, 1896/97. The house was enlarged by W. Baring Bingham in 1881–2. He dressed his servants in green livery. It was owned by the Revd W.N. Berkeley when this photograph was taken.

SOME OF THE STAFF AT CHARLTON LAWN on 28 May 1920. From left to right: the housemaid, Hilda Smith; the kitchen maid and the parlour maid; the coachman-gardener.

HOUSE IN THE TREE INN, Hayden's Elm, near Cheltenham. The porch of this 500 year-old coaching inn has recently been removed. It has long been a haunt of National Hunt racegoers. It is claimed that Maud of 'Maud's Elm' was taken from this inn.

THE OLD HOUSE IN THE TREE at Hayden, with the Tewkesbury Road in the foreground. The house, which no longer exists, gives its name to the public house there.

THE HOUSE IN THE TREE public house, Hayden, with the landlord Fred Hobbs and his wife, Ada, in the cart and two of their daughters with their bikes. Fred was landlord from 1910 to the 1930s.

THE CHILDREN'S CHUTE AT THE EVERSFIELD TEA AND PLEASURE GROUNDS. Bishop's Cleeve. Sunday school outings from Cheltenham always visited this adventurous playground.

SECTION TWO

Shops and Industries

VIEW OF MACHINE SHOP, H.H. MARTYN. The firm started in 1900 as memorial sculptors and moved to the Lansdown Station area in 1906.

PLANE ASSEMBLY IN WINTER GARDENS, H.H. Martyn (top and bottom).

CAR ASSEMBLY, H.H. Martyn.

PLANE ASSEMBLY, H.H. Martyn. By 1918 they produced complete aircraft.

WING ASSEMBLY, H.H. Martyn.

WOMEN SEWING WINGS. Those standing up worked in pairs, one on each side, passing a foot-long needle to each other. H.H. Martyn.

STATUE CONSTRUCTION, H.H. Martyn.

DECORATIVE WORK, H.H. Martyn. With 500 employees they built up a world-wide reputation in sculpture, carving, in stone and metal. The Speaker's chair, the Despatch Boxes and other interior work in the House of Commons were their work.

SCULPTURE WORK, H.H. Martyn.

WOODWORK, H.H. Martyn.

FOUNDRY, H.H. Martyn.

METAL WORKSHOP, H.H. Martyn.

H.H. MARTYN FOUNDRY TEAM pouring molten bronze in unison for an Australian war memorial in the 1920s.

GLOUCESTERSHIRE AIRCRAFT CO.'s SUNNINGEND WORKS in 1907.

THE 'FAMOUS' in Bath Road, 1896. Founded in 1886, and moved to the High Street in 1896. This postcard has the following printed message on the reverse: 'We have Transferred our Branch in the BATH ROAD to Mr. C. BARRETT and ask for him a continuance of the support given to us. "The Famous", Regd. Tailors & Outfitters 350–1 High Street, Cheltenham. Established 1886. Closed Wednesday, 1 o'clock. Proprietor: A.N. COLE'. Mr Cole had bought the shop and it has remained in his family ever since.

W. PALMER & CO., Furniture and General Dealers, Fairview Road, 1920s. Today the building is T.K. Motors garage. The little girl is leaning on a postman's delivery trike, altered for other purposes by Mr Palmer.

CHELTINE FOOD, on the site behind the present Public Library.

THE BAKERY IN TIVOLI, c. 1912/13.

LOCKE & SONS CATERING SHOP, Clarence Street. Weddings, ball suppers, and garden parties were among their specialities. The Cheltenham & Gloucester Building Society occupies the site today.

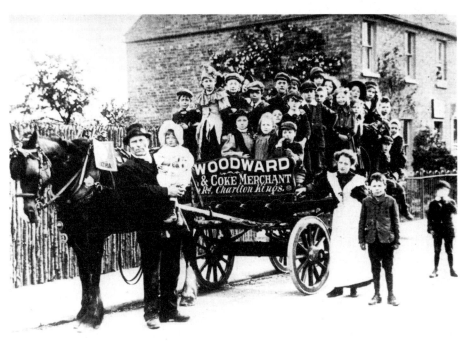

WOODWARD, Coal & Coke Merchant of Charlton Kings, on a special occasion.

YATE'S & SONS, Seed Growers and Bulb Importers, about to send a large order of seeds to New Zealand. College Road is on the far left and near the shop is the High Street entrance to Sandford Park.

THE DOBELL & CO. LTD. warehouse and horse-drawn delivery vehicles. The building was at the junction of the High Street and Gloucester Road.

BARNBY BENDALLS, the furniture and removal firm of St George's Place, sometime in the 1920s. The firm started in 1839. Photograph by Parsons of Rodney Terrace.

W. SEABRIGHT WILCOX, BRIDGE SHAVING SALOON, Townsend Place, near the Lower High Street bridge at the corner of Swindon Street, 1907.

RECEIVING OFFICE AND ENTRANCE.

ONE OF THE IRONING ROOMS

ENGINE ROOM.

SECTION OF WASH HOUSE.

DRYING GROUND (4,000 SUPER FEET IN EXTENT).

CHELTENHAM HYGIENIC LAUNDRY CO.,
335 HIGH ST. (Opposite Grammar School),
Nat. Tel. 933   **CHELTENHAM**

EVERYTHING in this world is own d by somebody—with one exception, the Air, and with the arrival of Airships in the near future this looks like being monopolised and served out to us by Meter, like Gas, Water, and Electric Light. So whilst it is yet free, the Management of THE HYGIENIC LAUNDRY is using an unlimited supply in Washing your Linen. It has hitherto been impossible to create sufficient Active Oxygen (which is the soul of washing), but now the problem has been solved, and New Machines have been erected at the above premises which turn out Linen of a Dazzling Whiteness without the slightest detriment or wear and tear of the fabric. With Flannels, nothing has ever been invented to beat our grandmothers' system, which is retained. But in the Ironing, science is to the fore, and machines to turn out Sheets, Table Cloths, etc., at the rate of 80 to 100 per hour are in use. In fact, the management have the Last Word in Laundry Appliances. They do not lay claim to be the largest, but claim to be the Best Appointed in the West of England. Work can be collected and delivered spotlessly clean in a few hours to any part of the district. Free. We of course mean the collection and delivery is free, but a moderate charge is made for getting up your Linen, so as to keep us clear of the Prevention of Corruption Act.

CHELTENHAM HYGIENIC LAUNDRY CO., 335 High Street, opposite the Grammar School. (1) Receiving Office. (2) One of the ironing rooms. (3) Engine Room. (4) Section of the Wash House. (5) Drying Ground, '4000 super feet in extent'. The machines used *Active Oxygen* to turn out 'Linen of a Dazzling Whiteness without the slightest detriment or wear and tear of the fabric .... In the Ironing, science is to the fore, and machines turn out Sheets, Table Cloths. etc., at the rate of 80 to 100 per hour .... Collection and delivery free.'

'THE WEST OF ENGLAND TOILET SALOON', Messrs Stibbs & Son's Hairdressing Saloon, North Street, next to the Wilts and Dorset Bank, June 1912. 'Any of our gentlemen readers who have not already visited it should do so at the first opportunity, as the luxurious comfort of their American Shaving Chairs (the only ones in Cheltenham) cannot be fully appreciated without a trial.'

LESLIE PAYNTER'S BATH STREET MOTOR CYCLIST'S MECCA, 1926. He was the agent for BSA, Norton, Douglas, New Imperial, Francis Barnett, etc.

FRANCIS HUGHES (on left) outside his Montpellier Cycle Depot, Montpellier Arcade, c. 1930. Beside him is Mr Marth and on the right, Charlie Evans.

BIRCHLEY & FORESHEW, the cycle-makers' shop, Henrietta Street. Notice the advertisement on the left offering cycle lessons.

JOHN FISHER & SONS, Winchcomb Street, before they merged with Sharpe's.

SHARPE & FISHER LTD'S PAINT AND WALLPAPER DEPTS, in Albion Street. John Charles Fisher, who
founded the firm with Thomas Sharpe in 1912, is on the left in the doorway.

SHARPE & FISHER LTD'S PITTVILLE STREET SHOP in the 1920s. It had been opened in 1914.

SHARPE & FISHER LTD'S MAIN PITTVILLE STREET SHOP which opened in the mid-1920s.

MELIAS, the grocers, in St George's Place, opposite the present Sainsbury's, 1925.

JOHN CARLSON outside his shop, Carlson's, 306 High Street, c. 1918.

BATH ROAD, 1906. S. Clark's grocery store is on the right.

WOODWARD'S DELIVERY VEHICLE, C. 1909. Eric Woodward who was connected with this firm was a well-known conductor.

A.E. WOODWARD'S MUSIC SHOP in the Strand, c. 1910.

JOHN LANCE & CO. LTD. in the High Street adjoined the present Boots. This photograph was taken before 1910. The company later joined with Shirers to become Shirer & Lances.

ST JOHN'S PHARMACY, Hewlett Road. Notice the maid cleaning the window from the balcony.

GEORGE'S, High Street, stood on the present site of W.H. Smith's. It is likely that it was decorated for the Coronation of Edward VII in this photograph.

E.L. WARD, the outfitters, High Street, stood where Littlewoods does today. Photographed in around 1910.

THE ORIGINAL CHELTENHAM & GLOUCESTER BUILDING SOCIETY OFFICE, c. 1909/1910.

J. URSELL'S GROCERY STORES, Elm View House, 128 Swindon Road, c. 1924. Jack and Myra Ursell are shown with Mr Ursell's brother. Today the shop is *Anemone*, the flower shop.

PART OF AN ADVERTISEMENT FOR H.E. STEELE'S GARAGE, High Street, on the site of the present C & A store, c. 1910.

COATES' FUNERAL SERVICE CORTÈGE in St Paul's, 1926/7.

SECTION THREE

Transport

GWR MALVERN ROAD STATION ENGINE SHED before Sharpe & Fisher took it over as their Glass and Timber Division. Their head office stands on the station site.

MALVERN ROAD GREAT WESTERN RAILWAY STATION, C. 1910.

LECKHAMPTON GREAT WESTERN RAILWAY STATION, Kingham Line, C. 1910.

CHARLTON KINGS' STATION SIGN, Easter holidays, 1927. A family picnic outing in full school uniform!

HIGH STREET RAILWAY SIDINGS, Tewkesbury Road. No date.

CHELTENHAM FLYER'S 1000th RUN, March, 1933. The world's fastest train which ran from Cheltenham to Paddington, with its driver G. Burgess and fireman, C. Brown, in 2 hours 23½ minutes, averaging 81.6 m.p.h. between Swindon and London. It is shown at Gloucester station.

TRAM TERMINUS, LECKHAMPTON, c. 1907. Notice the advertisement for John Lance's, whose shop is shown in the 'Shops' section.

CLEEVE HILL TRAM TERMINUS AND CAFE, 1906. The *Opera House* had Leah Kleschna performing according to the tram's advertisement board.

CHELTENHAM TRAM NO 18, C. 1907.

CHELTENHAM & DISTRICT LIGHT RAILWAY LORRY with solid tyres, 1923.

CHELTENHAM & DISTRICT LIGHT RAILWAY STAFF, 1927.

CHELTENHAM & DISTRICT LIGHT RAILWAY'S EARLY MOTORISED BUS. Date unknown.

CHELTENHAM & DISTRICT LIGHT RAILWAY PRE-WAR RENAULT VAN AND DELIVERY STAFF outside the company's North Street building, 1922.

EARLY MOTORISED PARCELS AND LUGGAGE DELIVERY SERVICE VAN photographed outside the Tram Terminus, beside Lansdown Station. The Parcel Office was in North Street.

J. & A. TOMBS, Van Builders, 56–58 Fairview Road, 1929.

THE 'TOAST RACK' OPEN BUS decorated for the Silver Jubilee of 1935. It took its nickname from its resemblance to a toast rack.

Black & White Motorways Limited
Motor Coach Station, Cheltenham Spa.

BLACK & WHITE MOTORWAYS LTD. MOTOR COACH STATION, before the covered section was built, 1900.

THE BLACK & WHITE MOTORWAYS LTD. COACH STATION before the covered section was built, 1929. The Georgian house was adapted for this use in 1931. The two coaches in the foreground are Bristol 'Two Tonners', while the one under the tree is a Leyland-bodied 'Tiger' which had a toilet on board for passenger convenience.

A BLACK & WHITE LEYLAND CUB 20-SEATER TOURING COACH beside Pittville Lake, 1934.

BLACK & WHITE MOTORWAYS LTD. Cafe, Car Park and Coach Station, 1949.

A BLACK & WHITE COACH used for the Cheltenham Boys' Orphanage tableaux in a carnival procession. No doubt vehicle registration buffs could date this one.

DE HAVILLAND 'MOTH', price £595, supplied by Westgate Motors, Gloucester, for the Westgate Motor Club Aerodrome, 1930/31. The airfield stood where the Dowty-Rotol factory stands opposite the present Staverton Airport. The field was owned by a farmer, A.W. King.

Events

CHARLTON KINGS' 'GREETINGS TO THE PRINCE OF WALES' ARCH for his visit in May, 1897. Franklin's, the butchers and the London Inn. Mr Franklin and his neighbour Mr Walker, the baker and corn chandler, are shown.

MERRYWEATHER GEM FIRE-ENGINE, made in 1898, and presented to the town in 1904 by Mrs Theobalds. The practice demonstration is in Montpellier Gardens, with the bandstand in view.

ONE OF MRS ROSE'S TABLEAUX in which three members of the Martyn family took part.

MRS ROSE'S PAGEANT CAST outside the Pump Room. Mrs Martyn as the Duchess of Kent in the centre.

THE PRINCIPAL CHARACTERS IN THE PAGEANT outside the Pump Room.

JAMES HOLE, market gardener, as *John Higgs* in the famous 1908 pageant.

ACME FLOORING AND PAVING CO. at work in Cheltenham, January 1905.

EMPIRE DAY in Cheltenham, 24 May 1909. Tea given by Major and Mrs Percy Shewell in the Winter Garden to 'elder scholars from all the elementary schools in Cheltenham'.

ODDFELLOWS' CONFERENCE at the Winter Gardens, 1909.

THE CORPORATION TEAM, who came second, face Dr Hayman, the judge of the St John Ambulance Competition, Montpellier Baths, 1910. The Police Team won the Shewell Shield; third were St Peter's Team and fourth, the Friendly Societies.

FINDING WORK FOR THE UNEMPLOYED – cleaning out Pittville Lake, January 1909. The sludge was dug out to a depth of four feet and transferred to Mr Maby's field by trolleys.

CHELTENHAM TO CARDIFF BY AIRSHIP, July 1910. Mr Willow's flight from Montpellier Gardens in his airship, *Willows II*. (4) He is talking to Mr Dale and Mr H.E. Steele. (5) He discusses being followed by cars with Mr Dale and Mr F. Norman.

CORONATION DAY BONFIRE, Leckhampton, 1911.

SHOWELL'S BREWERY OUTING TO ASCOT, June 1914. Fine weather was essential for coach outings then! The brewery was at the corner of St Paul's Street South.

UNVEILLING OF THE MEMORIAL TO DR E.A. WILSON by Sir C. R. Markman in the Promenade, 9 July 1914. Photograph by J.W. Hack of Suffolk Road, Cheltenham.

FORTY CHELTONIAN EMIGRANTS TO CANADA leave from the Midland Railway Station on the night of 7 April 1913. This flashlight photograph shows them leaving on the 9.30p.m. train for Liverpool.

DIGGING THE SLUDGING TANK at Hayden Sewage Works, near Fiddlers Green, just before the First World War. The men are 14s-a-week farm labourers attracted by the £1-a-week wages offered.

A 6-HOSEPIPE, 45-GALLON NEW LEYLAND FIRE ENGINE being tested at Pittville Park lake on 11 October 1923. The mayor took the opportunity for a ride.

DARING JEWEL ROBBERY IN CHELTENHAM, 2 February 1922. With 'diabolical cleverness' a 30–35 year-old man entered Messrs Martin & Co., Promenade, squirted liquid in the assistant's eyes and snatched fifty uninsured diamond rings worth £2,000. The *Graphic's* reconstruction shows how he ran across to his motor cycle in County Court Lane and got away to the vicinity of the Midland Station, where he disposed of the ring tray. He had not been caught a week later.

CHELTENHAM CORPORATION SEWAGE FARMS wins two First prizes at the Hatherley & Reddings Show, 1923.

FRANK PALMER WITH HIS HOME-MADE MONOPLANE on Cleeve Hill, Good Friday, 1924. The propeller was powered by a Lloyd Chainless Bike frame placed in a reverse position; it achieved an average of 600 revs. per minute. Aided by Winchcombe Boy Scouts the plane flew 90 metres at 3 metres high, before nose-diving into the ground.

'BRITAIN'S SPEED RECORDS', the Palmer family's winning entry at the Gloucester and Fairford Carnivals in 1930. Underneath is a Cubitt car. The black bow on the front of 'Miss England' speedboat refers to the recent death of its owner while attempting a further record.

CYRIL PALMER ON HIS 'TALLEST MOTORBIKE', 14 ft. high, in 1935. After a good circuit of the field, he was knocked off by a low loudspeaker cable.

CHELTENHAM'S GREAT HOSPITAL CARNIVAL, June 1934. Opening ceremony by Lady Helena Gibbs of Tetbury in front of the Queen's Hotel complete with the Crimean guns.

SKATING AT PITTVILLE, December 1935. A 'serpent' of College boys.

THE FIRST BALL HELD BY THE CHELTENHAM YOUNG FARMERS CLUB, Town Hall, 1937.

THE FIRST CALF COMPETITION, Cheltenham Young Farmers Club, Gloucester Market, 1938.

SECTION FIVE

Church and Chapel

ST MATTHEW'S 'TIN' CHURCH, built in 1859 while work was being carried out at the parish church.

22 CHELTENHAM. — St. Matthew's Church. — LL.

ST MATTHEW'S CHURCH when it had a spire and postcards cost ½d to send. The photograph is a French one.

THE OPENING CEREMONY OF THE SALE OF WORK, St Peter's parish hall, Waterloo Street, 1907.

ST PAUL'S SALE OF WORK at the church hall in Milsom Street. Each year the event was given a theme and the congregation dressed up suitably. The Revd Mr Cave Moyle was the vicar.

ST PAUL'S BOYS' BRIGADE BIBLE CLASS, 1914. The curate is in the middle.

ST PAUL'S SUNDAY SCHOOL PARADE, which went round the town, 1931/32.

KING'S MESSENGERS, a church group which met fortnightly at the Grange with Miss Heberden for picnics outdoors or in the coach house if wet. Pageants were done in aid of Missions in the Grange garden.

ST MARK'S CHURCH CRICKET TEAM, 1937. A. Nottingham is on the right with his bat, while behind him, on the far right, is Mr Wheeler, secretary of the Holloway Society. Jesse Cripps is second from the right in the back row, while in the centre, with his cap on, is H. Evans, a director of Barnby Bendell. On the back left is Mr Edden, a carpenter at Peacocks and a churchwarden at St Mark's.

ST MARY'S PARISH CHURCH FOOTBALL TEAM. The rector is the Revd Mr Wilson on the right, and his curate, the Revd Mr Couch, is on the left.

THE REVD EDGAR NEALE (vicar of St Mary's, Charlton Kings, 1906–37), and his Choir XI, 1912. There were 24 boys and 18 men in the choir and they sung choral evensong six nights a week and had five practices in addition. The canon was a master of comic songs which he sung in his bass voice. He once said, 'St Mary's was famous for two things, its missionary interests, and the musical maniac it had for a vicar.' He once paid his boys' fines when they broke the china fittings on telegraph poles.

ALL SAINTS' CHURCH CHOIR, c. 1935. Centre third row, Dr A. Melville Cook, organist and choirmaster, later organist at Leeds Parish Church and Hereford Cathedral.

DR A. MELVILLE COOK when organist at All Saints' Church (1935–7), educated at King's School, Gloucester, assistant organist Gloucester Cathedral (1932–37), Leeds Parish Church and Hereford Cathedral, conductor of Halifax Choral Society, etc.

BETHESDA METHODIST CHURCH OUTING in the early 1900s.

BETHESDA METHODIST CRICKET TEAM, 1923.

SWINDON ROAD WESLEYAN CHAPEL, c. 1900.

ROYAL WELL METHODIST CHAPEL at the junction of St George's Road. It was closed in 1936 and was used as a car showroom for many years.

THE OPENING OF ST MARK'S METHODIST CHURCH, Gloucester Road by Mrs F.W. Brown of Arle Court Farm, 15 November 1911.

CHELTENHAM SALVATION ARMY BAND with Adjutant and Mrs Huish in the centre, 1910. The Colour Sergeant was Mr Richards.

SALVATION ARMY BAND FESTIVAL AT THE CITADEL Bath Road, 14 December 1940. Bandmaster R. Button is seated in the centre.

People

TELEGRAPH MESSENGERS posing just before the GPO moved from Clarence Street to the Promenade in 1877.

CHELTENHAM POSTMEN starting the Christmas delivery. 'Men who do *not* long for Christmas,' said the *Graphic's* caption, 1909.

CLEEVELY FAMILY OUTSIDE THORNTONVILLE, 1893. Ivy Cottage is just visible behind the chimneys.

FOUR BROTHERS IN THE FIRST GLOUCESTERSHIRE ROYAL ENGINEERS VOLUNTEERS' REGIMENT at camp, Fort Tregantle, 1904. They are all Cheltonians.

CHELTENHAM VOLUNTEERS IN THE FIRST GLOUCESTERSHIRE ROYAL ENGINEERS VOLUNTEER REGIMENT at camp, Fort Tregantle, 1904.

CHELTENHAM WORKING MEN'S CLUB third annual outing to the Lower Lode Hotel on the River Severn, 14 July 1906. The variety of their hats could almost rival a women's fashion show!

CHARLTON KINGS GWR STATION, 1912, with employees of the Urban District Council about to leave for St Gile's Fair, Oxford, on their annual outing.

COTSWOLD HOUNDS at Lilleybrook, date unknown.

FÊTE AT LILLEYBROOK, sometime before 1914.

INNER WHEEL FUND RAISING GARDEN PARTY, 1920s.

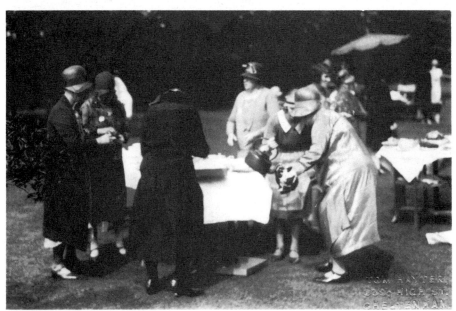

INNER WHEEL GARDEN PARTY, 1920s.

CHELTENHAM OPERATIC & DRAMATIC SOCIETY WEDDING between Rex Watson and Madeleine Martyn at Holy Apostles Church, 11 September 1928. Group photographed in the garden of Herne House.

THE GROOM WITH HIS FELLOW MALE SINGERS OF CODS at the Watson-Martyn wedding. Cecil Martyn is on the right and Arthur Cole, the director of music, on the left.

THE BRIDE WITH HER FELLOW FEMALE SINGERS OF CODS at the Watson-Martyn wedding.

CHELTENHAM GIRL GUIDES AND SCOUTS at the Garden Fête, Swindon Rectory, 7 July 1920.

CHELTENHAM COMPETITIVE MUSIC FESTIVAL, 1934. (1) Oriel School percussion band won the Boulton Challenge Cup. (2) Misses P. Burrows, M. Boyle, Cuthbert-Brown, winners of Janet Salisbury Silver Challenge Cup. (3) John Gilbert, accompanist. (4) J. Worster, second violin. (5) St Paul's College Male Voice Choir. (6) Piano competitors, Margery Ellis, Eileen Bussell, Muriel Vernon, I. Smith and Gilbert Smith. (7) Margery Deavin, first for 'cello. (8) Miss M. Kear, bronze medal for piano sight-reading. (9) Miss Norah Fell, Mrs Platt, Miss Esther Giller; front – Mrs L. McDermott, Miss Cuthbert-Brown, first for chamber music. (10) Mr and Mrs H.H. Chandler, Lewis Hann and Festival officials. (11) Cheltenham Ladies' Choir.

TWELFTH CHELTENHAM SCOUT TROOP, the Parish Church Troop, outside Thirleston Hall, 1912.

GLOUCESTERSHIRE SCOUT SWIMMING CHAMPIONS, first winners of the Marling Cup as overall champions, 1912–13. Trainer W. Ashfield in the rear, with J. Groves on his right and W. Johnson on the left. Front, from the left, Bill Tiver (holder of the Bouth Challenge Cup), R. Hogg and A. Harding.

GLOUCESTERSHIRE STANDARD leading the Sea Rangers' Church Parade, Montpellier Street, early 1940s. Marjorie Hyde (now Mrs Zebedee) holding the flag.

SEA RANGERS ON THE MARCH in Clarence Street, early 1940s, with Marjorie Hyde (now Mrs Zebedee) as 'marker'. Their HQ was Holy Apostles Church Hall.

SEA RANGERS COOKING BESIDE THEIR TENTS at Bredon, 1940s. From left to right: Barbara Gough, Muriel Churchman, Mavis Adams.

SAUSAGES FOR TEA! Sea Rangers at camp, Bredon, 1940s. Back row, left to right: Muriel Heath, Irene Gardner; front, Bridget Haden, Eileen Stabback.

'TOSSING OARS'. The Sea Rangers at their Bredon camp, 1940s. Cox, Muriel Heath; stroke, Bridget Haden; 3, Eileen Stabback; 2, Fay Piper; Bow, unknown. They kept their boats at Bathurst's, Tewkesbury.

A GARDEN PARTY at the home of Mr and Mrs E.L. Ward. A veritable feast of garden party hats! One for the ladies to date.

THE ENTIRE POPULATION OF SWINDON VILLAGE in the grounds of Swindon Hall, 1935.

GREAT WESTERN RAILWAY STAFF, St James' Station. Date unknown.

THE CHELTENHAM RABBIT CLUB in the 1940s. Mrs Nancy Morris is in the centre.

Schools and Colleges

THE DEVONSHIRE STREET BLUECOAT BOYS' SCHOOL, 1865.

CHELTENHAM COLLEGE OF ART on its original site near the rear of the Boys' Grammar School, c. 1909.

BOYS' GRAMMAR SCHOOL, High Street, on its original site now occupied by Sainsbury's, around 1909.

WORKMEN building the back of the Boys' Grammar School.

MANDOLIN GROUP, at Charlton Park Girls' School, School Road, 1909/10.

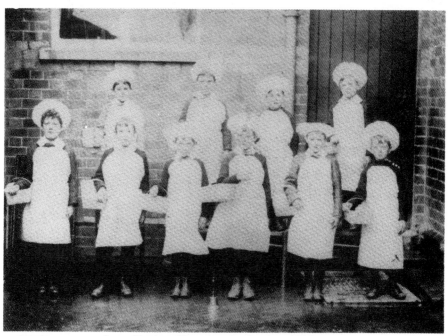

BLACKBERRYING PARTY from Charlton Kings local school, c. 1910.

CLASSES 6 AND 7, PARISH CHURCH BOYS SCHOOL, Devonshire Street, 1910. On the left is the rector, the Revd Fawcett, who was six foot, four inches tall. Headmaster Wheeler and his assistant are on the right.

H. WOODMAN AND J. BETHELL of the Parish Church School XV who both played for England v. Wales at Leicester on 1 March 1913.

THE PARISH CHURCH BOYS SCHOOL, Devonshire Street, in their bicentenary year, 1913. Their teacher was Mr G. Adam.

PARISH SCHOOL, Devonshire Street, the First Class, 1922.

HOLY APOSTLES SCHOOL, 1924.

HOLY APOSTLES SCHOOL, 1928.

ST PAUL'S SCHOOL, 1927.

ST PAUL'S SCHOOL, 1933, with Muriel Betteridge (née Miles) fourth from the left of the first standing row.

SWINDON ROAD (NOW ELMFIELD) SCHOOL HOCKEY TEAM, which won the town championship, 1929–30. Violet Vizard (née Davis) is seated on the far right. She got a black-eye when playing in a mixed match with the boys.

SWINDON ROAD (NOW ELMFIELD) SCHOOL COUNTRY DANCE TEAM. They won the county competition in 1929.

SWINDON ROAD SCHOOL, 1930. Standing, left to right: Mr Bristow, R. Herbert, R. Russell, P. Herbert, A. Taylor, F. Piff and the headmaster, Mr Hunnum. Seated: S. Attwood, R. Millington, W. Burford, P. Pearce, A. Roberts. In front: Moxey and R. Gapper. Staff are standing in the traditional 'protective' position for such photographs.

NAUNTON PARK INFANTS' SCHOOL, c. 1930.

NAUNTON PARK BOYS' SCHOOL, Class III, 1928.

ST MARK'S SCHOOL, 1931. Small classes in those days!

LECKHAMPTON JUNIOR SCHOOL, 1935.

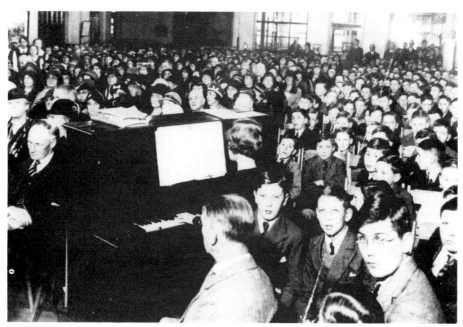

CENTRAL SCHOOL FOR BOYS' SPEECH DAY in the mid 1930s.

The Two World Wars

GLOUCESTERSHIRE HUSSARS, CHELTENHAM TROOP, during the Great War.

THE CHELTENHAM 'HOME GUARD' of the Great War.

LEEK PLANTING sometime during the First World War at Arlebrook Gardens, now the site of Lex Mead Ltd. The house is where Quicksave is today.

SWINDON LADIES' WORK COMMITTEE, 1914. Hats were all the rage in those days!

CHARLTON KINGS' GUIDES harvesting at Southern Delabere during the First World War.

TWO GERMAN PRISONERS helping with the beer delivery to House in the Tree public house during World War I.

THE KITCHEN AND SCULLERY STAFF AT THE ROTUNDA which was the 'Soldiers' Home' in 1915. On the left is the Rotunda's custodian, while in the centre of the back row is schoolmaster Percy Crowther, who acted as cook. He was the scoutmaster of the Twelfth Cheltenham Scout Troop, some of whom are also shown. Their task was to go round to local 'big houses' and collect large tins of rice pudding which they had to balance on their bikes. Misses Wethered and Harford assisted Mr Crowther.

A MILITARY FUNERAL held during the First World War in Cheltenham. This photograph and the next refer to two different funerals. Privates Jerrom and Callaghan were buried on April 29 and Privates Fenton, Turner and Warren on May 4 1918. These Australian soldiers had died at Voluntary Aid Hospitals in Cheltenham after being gassed in the German offensives of March 1918.

THE TROOPS PRECEDING THE COFFIN at the military funeral. Notice they are carrying their arms in the 'reverse' position.

MARK 4 TANK 285 at Westal Green. It was presented to the town in May 1919, for meritorious war savings. It was escorted from the GWR station by Dean Close corps band. Its captain said there were lady and gentleman tanks and *285* was a lady, being difficult to handle. In fact a 'lady' only had a machine gun and no 'male' six-pounder guns in the sponsons. 'Tank Week' followed and raised £4,549. It was vandalised in later years and taken for scrap in World War II.

THE WAR MEMORIAL in the Promenade photographed the Sunday after its unveiling.

ENGELFONTAINE, the French village which suffered in the Great War, and which Cheltenham adopted in 1921. The town's MP visited the village and reported on its needs. Top right is the town hall and centre, the girls' school.

CHELTENHAM ARP (AIR RAID PRECAUTION) PERSONNEL taking part in a demonstration and parade, Pittville Park, early 1940s.

CHELTENHAM SHOPFITTING COMPANY VOLUNTEERS removing railings from Royal Well Church, St George's Road, July 1940.

PART OF ONE DAY'S COLLECTION IN RESPONSE TO THE ALUMINIUM APPEAL FOR THE AIRCRAFT INDUSTRY at the WVS emergency store, 7 Albion Street, July 1940.

AIR DEFENCE CADETS MAKING A HOUSE-TO-HOUSE ALUMINIUM COLLECTION in the Park district, July 1940.

KEEP-FIT DISPLAY in aid of the YMCA Canteen Appeal Fund by members of Cheltenham and Prestbury classes at the Lypiatts, Lansdown Road, August 1940.

GAS-MASK DRILL for St Paul's Infant School. The *Cheltenham Chronicle* reported that 'they are provided with a splendid set of shelters in the square adjoining their school in front of St Paul's Church', 13 July 1940.

COMMUNAL FRUIT-PRESERVING AND JAM-MAKING CENTRE at Marlborough House, Cheltenham, one of the town's eight centres that opened in August 1940.

CHILDREN'S GARDEN SALE FOR THE HURRICANE FUND. Ten-year-old Jean Smith of 255 Prestbury Road and eight-year-old Alan Ventura of 249 hold the bazaar in the garden of 255. They raised £4 17s. 9d. towards the £7,000 cheque sent to the Ministry of Aircraft Production in September, 1940.

MILITARY WEDDINGS WERE SOON A FEATURE. Captain A. E. Wilkinson, son of Lt-Col. Wilkinson, married Pamela Woollcombe, daughter of Major H. Woollcombe-Jackson and grand-daughter of Dr. R. Kirkland of 'Nouvelle', Lansdown Crescent, at Christ Church in September 1940.

ROOM FOR 200 in the large air-raid shelter made by Mr and Mrs Arthur Bailey in the old
brewery cellars of their premises in Sherborne Street, September 1940.

A 1,000 TON STACK OF RESERVE COAL in Cheltenham. One of the reserver dumps only to be
used in dire necessity arranged by G. G. Marshland, the local Fuel Controller, October 1940.

FIRST-AID PARTY at the Elms, Swindon Road, Cheltenham, October 1940.

CHELTENHAM'S WAR WEAPONS' WEEK DISPLAY November 1940. A Bren gun carrier.

CHELTENHAM HOME GUARD CHURCH PARADE, November 1940. 1. Gasworks Contingent. 2. Charlton Kings Platoon. 3. Hatherley members. 4. Cheltenham College Band. 5. Leckhampton Platoon. 7. Tewkesbury Contingent. 8. Charlton Kings members. 9. Muncipal Company, with Lt-Col. Tudor Fitzjohn in front.

WAR WEAPONS WEEK DISPLAY with a 3.7 AA gun between the two Crimean guns outside the Queen's Hotel, November 1940. Perhaps the last photograph of the Crimean guns before they were removed for their metal.

YMCA WORKER Miss Joy Bagnall with her miniature mobile canteen. Her mother also drove a canteen.

ST MARK'S METHODIST KNITTING AND SEWING CIRCLE contributing to the war effort in the 1940s.

THE LANSDOWN STATION YMCA CANTEEN FOR THE TROOPS in the 1940s.

THE VOLUNTARY WORKERS' PARADE at Montpellier Gardens prior to inspection by Queen Mary in the 1940s.

THE BLACK & WHITE GEORGIAN HOUSE COACH STATION receives a direct hit on 11 December 1940.

110th GENERAL HOSPITAL, US ARMY, Ullenwood Court, built for 3,000 in 1939.

110th GENERAL HOSPITAL. The huts were for the wounded white troops and the tents for the coloured troops.

US TROOPS, wounded at the Battle of the Bulge, arriving in a hospital train at Leckhampton Station, to be to taken to 110th General Hospital (Ullenwood Court).

AMBULANCES lined up at 110th General Hospital, Ullenwood.

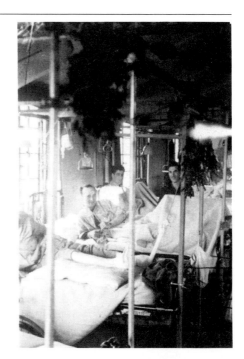

ORTHOPAEDIC WARD, 110th General Hospital, Ullenwood, Christmas 1944.

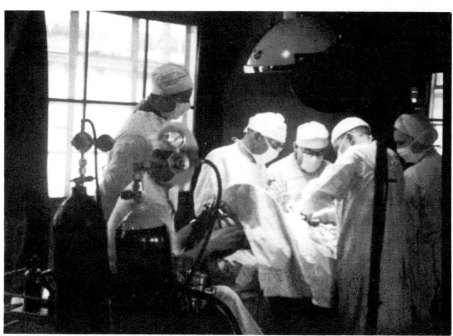

OPERATING THEATRE, 110th General Hospital, Ullenwood, during World War II.

HAYDEN FARM ANTI-AIRCRAFT BATTERY opposite the House in the Tree Inn in the Second World War. A Camp 'Ditty' of 495 (M) H.A.A. Battery 'B' was called *Unexplored Territory*: 'I have just returned from my latest expedition. This time into the unexplored territory known as Haydens Elm. Venturing far into the depths where it was thought no man had ever been I came upon the natives. They were born very young and very primitive. Chief of the tribe was called *No Glasses Drew* and his squaw *Empty Quick Drew*. To *No Glasses Drew*'s famous settlement the natives flocked of an evening led by *Long Sitting Drink Davidson* and *Standing Bull Ping Pong Collier* wearing strange marks on their sleeves, another *White Chief* came over on his fairy cycle . . . . After their fill of *No Glasses Drew* firewater, they all assembled on the grass and would chant native songs with curious titles such as "Detachments Bong, Bong, Rear" . . .'

ANTI-AIRCRAFT BATTERY opposite the House in the Tree.

SECTION NINE

Sport

ST PHILIP'S QUOIT CLUB, 1901.

CHELTENHAM CROQUET TOURNAMENT, Charlton Park, June 1902.

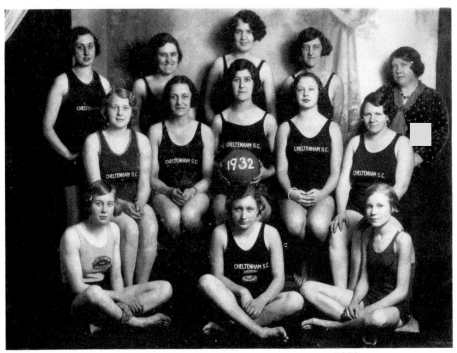

WOMEN'S TEAM OF THE CHELTENHAM SWIMMING AND WATER POLO CLUB, 1932.

COLIN LEWIS, founder member of the Cheltenham Swimming Club who swam backstroke in the 1908 Olympic Games.

CHELTENHAM SWIMMING AND WATER POLO CLUB with the trophies it won in 1933.

ST PAUL'S UNITED FOOTBALL TEAM, 1920s. Mr Norris, the headmaster of St Paul's Practising School (where St Paul's students did their teaching practice) is in the centre. On his right is A. Nottingham.

SUNNINGEND FOOTBALL TEAM in 1925/26. Arthur Clark's father is sporting a typical cap of the day.

UCAL FOOTBALL TEAM, London Road.

THE FIRST DOWTY RUGBY TEAM, the 1938–39 Aircraft Components Team, captain N.L. Hanson.

CHELTENHAM MOTOR CLUB'S MOTORBIKE FOOTBALL, 1947. Among those playing are Sam Barnet, Ron Partridge, Edgar Marshall and Bert Hulin. They played Stroud, Gloucester, Coventry and Northants, using a normal size ball. They played at the Albion Street Athletic Ground before crowds of 2,600. The sport dwindled when it was transferred to Whaddon football ground. Mainly scramble-type machines were used.

CHELTENHAM MOTOR CLUB'S FOOTBALL TEAM, 1950. Left to right: Max Finch, Peter Rees, Ron Partridge, Sam Barnet, Edgar Marshall, Tommy Rowles and George Stannard.

'OUTCASTS' DARTS TEAM at the White Horse, Tewkesbury Road, closed in 1946. From left: Mr Butler (landlord), Tom Higgs, Bill Sypher, Ernie Clutterbuck, Les Williams, G. Belcher, Shady Smith, Jock Midglade, Jack Smith. Sitting from left: captain Sean Goodhall, Frank Piff, Bill Burford, A. Smith.

'OUTCASTS' at the Golden Cross, on the corner of Townsend Street, which closed in 1960. Left: Jim Clifford (landlord), Tom Higgs, Frank Piff, Jack Smith, Bill Burford, Les Williams. Sitting: Guss Stone, Bill Sypher, captain Sean Goodhall, Jack Brown.

SECTION TEN

Entertainment

CHELTENHAM SPA MILITARY BAND, under Archie Coates (undertaker of Henrietta Street), at the Armistice Sunday Parade in the Promenade, 1926. Most of the players had served in the First World War. The 'Thirsty Three' were members. They used to practice in a room above the coffin shop. Behind them are R.F. Beard's, Nixon's the china shop, Maison Kunz, the high-class Swiss confectioner, and Slade's shoe shop.

THE MARTINIES, a Cheltenham group well known in the early years of the Second World War.

RAINBOW CONCERT PARTY, 1935. Violet Vizard (née Davis), right seated, did a *Gracie Field's* turn and a *Football-watching* turn.

H.H. MARTYN'S CONCERT PARTY during the First World War. They performed at the New Court Hotel.

H.H. MARTYN'S CONCERT PARTY performing a 'mock military wedding' during one of their performances.

THE NEW KINEMA, WINTER GARDEN, with *The Devil's Maze* on show, c. 1929/30. The manager was Eric Shenton and the lessee, Shakespeare Shenton.

H.G. BEARD'S THE PICTURE HOUSE, North Street, showing *Rough Romance* and *Three Days to Live*, July 1931.

THE PICTURE HOUSE STAFF, 16 July 1931. Left, Sid Williams, chief projectionist; centre, E.C. Ball, second projectionist; right, 'Rewind boy', Herbert.

GILL SMITH'S HIPPODROME, with its twice nightly performances, 1914.

PIPER'S PERFORMING BIRDS.

EDGAR PIPER'S PERFORMING BIRDS, 1920s. He made all his own props for his charity shows. The birds rode on swinging boats, see-saws and this roundabout. He was a familiar figure in the Promenade with his tricycle loaded with birds and animals for sale. Once a tortoise escaped and survived being run over by a car.

THE DOWTY PLAYERS' CAST FOR 'WHEN WE ARE MARRIED'. Back row, left to right: Mr Wiggins, John Fryer (producer), Mr Clayton, Jimmy James, Ken Walter, Len Basher, Frank Pearson. Front row: Iris Trower, Peggy Ostler, Win Hyde, Joan Warner, Miss Summers, Miss Russell, Jene Taylor.

'WHEN WE ARE MARRIED', was the Dowty Players' first production, staged at St Gregory's Hall, Cheltenham, 22–23 May 1944. From left to right: Miss Summers as Mrs Parker, Iris Trower (Lottie), Joan Warner (Mrs Helliwell) and Win Hyde (Mrs Soppitt). They all worked at the Aircraft Components Ltd., Arle Court. Mr (later Sir) George Dowty gave the ladies bouquets on the last night and took the company out to dinner. The producer was John Fryer, a professional actor. The company was one of the first to use the Playhouse when it ceased to be a swimming pool.

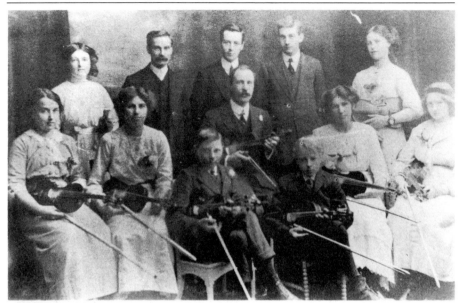

MARTIN'S WHITE ROSE ORCHESTRA, c. 1915.

JACK MANN ON THE XYLOPHONE AND RONNIE PLEYDELL ON THE VIOLIN, late 1920s. Jack worked in Dale Forty's gramophone department, and Ronnie, son of Mr Pleydell the pork butcher, played in Hector Davies' band.

BILLY DEREK ORCHESTRA in the Town Hall, 1932. It was then the resident orchestra at the Plough Hotel. Billy's real name was Gil Sparrow. His father was chef at George's Restaurant, Upper High Street, now W.H. Smith's. Frank Betteridge is at the piano, with Ewart Pitt, double bass, Jack Carpenter, drums, Jack Mann, xylophone, Eric Mundy, trumpet, Frank Cheers and Hubert Bastin, saxophones and Fred Colley, trombone.

THE ASTORIA DANCE BAND, Town Hall, 1927.

THE CHELTENHAM CHORAL SOCIETY in the 'Bells of Thanksgiving' Pageant at the Town Hall just after the Second World War. Mr Islwyn-Jones, the conductor is in the centre. The pageant marked the achievement of victory and peace.